CW00890979

# Shopify Ecommerce Mastery

Uncover the Secrets to Make Money
Without Spending a Single Penny on
Inventory

**Robert Hill**

# Table of Contents

**Introduction** ...................................................................1

What Is Shopify? ................................................ 1

Features And Benefits................................................ 2

Pros And Cons Of The Shopify Platform.................................. 3

   Advantages Of Shopify ................................................ 3

   Disadvantages Of Shopify................................................ 4

Things To Consider Before Starting A Shopify Store ...................... 5

   Questions To Help Plan Your Shopify Niche Store ..................... 6

   Real-World, Digital Or Services And Subscription Models ........ 7

   Niche Planning................................................ 7

   Store Design................................................ 7

   Order Fulfillment ................................................ 8

   Payment Methods ................................................ 8

**Chapter 1: How To Choose A Shopify Theme** ...................9

Shopify Options You Might Not Be Aware Of .............................. 10

   Customizing A Shopify Theme................................................ 10

   How To Choose................................................ 11

An Overview Of The Shopify App Store ................................. 11

Making The Most Use Of Shopify................................................ 13

   You Need To Design A Website ................................................ 14

   You Need To Incorporate And Secure Payment Gateways...... 15

   You Need To Fulfill Orders................................................ 15

Shopify Takes Care Of A Million Details ................................... 16

**Chapter 2: Ideas For Selling Physical Products On A Subscription**

**Basis** ................................................................................. 17

Some Tips For Getting More Members On Your Membership Site

................................................................................................. 19

Make It Sound Exciting ................................................. 20

Offer Levels Of Membership .................................... 20

Free Trial ........................................................................ 21

Recurring Passive Income Is The Ideal Business Model .............. 21

What Is Passive Recurring Income? .................................. 22

**Chapter 3: Profiting From Any Ecommerce Store** ...................... 24

Why A Cheap Item Can Make A Massive Difference .................. 25

Increasing Ecommerce Your Sales .................................... 26

Use A Red 'Buy Now' Button ................................... 26

Make Multiple Bundles At Different Price Points .................... 26

Sell Some Very Cheap Items ..................................... 27

Offer Free Samples ..................................................... 28

**Chapter 4: Using Affiliates To Sell More** ................................... 29

What Is An Affiliate Program? ........................................ 29

How To Set Up Affiliate Programs ................................. 30

Using Content Marketing For Your Shopify Store ...................... 31

What Is Content Marketing? ........................................ 31

**Chapter 5: Getting Stock Photos For Your Shopify Store**............**33**

Where To Find Stock Photos Of Products ...................................... 34

Stock Photo Websites .............................................................. 34

Ask The Manufacturer............................................................. 35

Using Pinterest To Make Sales In Your Shopify Store ................. 35

**Chapter 6: How Shopify Pays Store Owners** ...............................**38**

Shopify Funds Transfer............................................................ 39

How Does Shopify Support Work?............................................. 40

**Chapter 7: Brick-And-Mortar Store Work Hand-In-Hand With Shopify** ........................................................................................**43**

Let Your Real-World Customers Know........................................ 44

Offer Free In-Store Pickup........................................................ 44

Never Miss An Opportunity To Advertise ................................... 45

How Do Taxes Work On Shopify ................................................ 45

Sales Tax ........................................................................... 46

Income Tax ........................................................................ 47

Setting Up Product Variants With Shopify.................................. 47

How To Set Up Product Variants ............................................ 49

**Chapter 8: Growing Your Ecommerce Business** ..........................**50**

Continually Build On Your SEO And Keep Up With The Latest Trends............................................................................................ 51

Look For Viral Opportunities..................................................... 51

Always Be Evolving ........................................................... 52

Marketing Your Shopify Website .................................... 52

    Social Media Marketing............................................. 53

    Great Customer Service............................................. 54

    Build Expertise ........................................................... 55

**Chapter 9: Building A Brand That People Will Want To Buy From 56**

What Is A Brand?........................................................... 57

Communicating Your Brand ........................................ 58

Pricing And Positioning Your Items To Increase Sales ................ 59

    Using Contrast ........................................................... 60

    Selling One Cheap Item ............................................. 61

**Conclusion**.................................................................... **63**

How Businesses Make This Mistake All The Time........................ 65

**Checklist**....................................................................... **67**

**ECOMMERCE MASTERY** ............................................... **73**

Introduction ...................................................................... 75

Choosing A Profitable Niche ........................................... 76

Finding Your Passion ........................................................ 80

Going Deep........................................................................ 82

Sourcing Products ............................................................ 84

Drop Shipping.................................................................... 85

Buying Wholesale ............................................................ 87

Creating Your Own Products ........................................... 88

Marketing Your Store...................................................... 90

Have A USP..................................................................... 91

Social Media................................................................... 94

    Facebook .................................................................. 94

    Instagram .................................................................. 96

    Pinterest .................................................................... 97

    Other Social Networks ............................................. 98

**Conclusion** ................................................................**100**

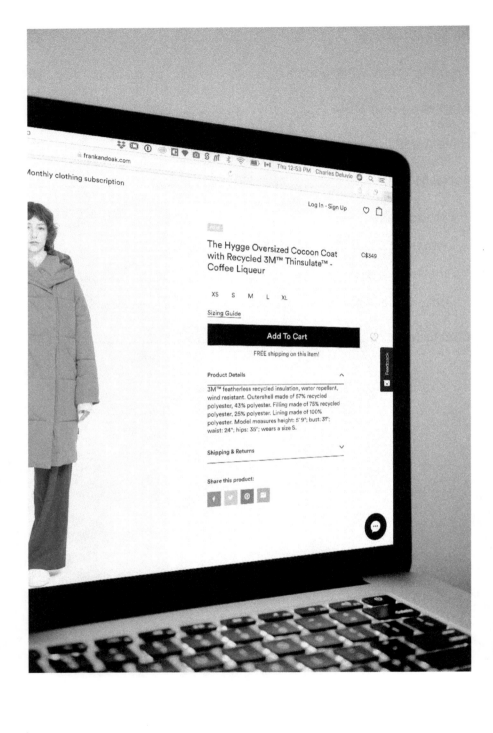

Log In - Sign Up

The Hygge Oversized Cocoon Coat
with Recycled 3M™ Thinsulate™ -
Coffee Liqueur

C$349

XS   S   M   L   XL

Sizing Guide

**Add To Cart**

FREE shipping on this item!

Product Details ∧

3M™ featherless recycled insulation, water repellent,
wind resistant. Outershell made of 57% recycled
polyester, 43% polyester. Filling made of 75% recycled
polyester, 25% polyester. Lining made of 100%
polyester. Model measures height: 5' 9"; bust: 31";
waist: 24"; hips: 35"; wears a size S.

Shipping & Returns ∨

Share this product:

Feedback

# Introduction

**If you want to add an ecommerce store to your website and start selling more products, then using Shopify to create an online shop is a great option.**

In this introduction, we will look at some of the things that make this such a good choice and at how you can make the most from it.

## What Is Shopify?

Shopify is an ecommerce store builder that allows you to sell any kind of item from your website, whether it is a physical product, a digital product, or a subscription.

Shopify is also what is known as a 'hosted' solution. This means that you do not need your own domain and you do not need to install it yourself. Rather, you just create a profile and set up your store that way and link to it from your website.

This is one of the first advantages of Shopify – it is incredibly quick, easy and reliable. You can create your store in a few clicks which takes just a few minutes. At the same time, you do not need to worry about your hosting provider going down or your site getting bogged down with traffic.

## Features and Benefits

On the face of it, you would think that Shopify would be less flexible owing to its hosted nature. Actually though, Shopify gets around this by letting you install a large number of paid and free themes as well as countless apps that extend the power of your store.

This means for instance that you can create a member only store, you can create a membership website, you can charge recurring payments, you can sell digital products and you can even integrate your site easily with your shop by using widgets.

Then there is the option to add your products to your Facebook page or to create an app!

Best of all, it is actually very affordable to begin with – so this really is the easiest way to start selling products from your site!

# Pros and Cons Of The Shopify Platform

Shopify is one of the greatest platforms ever created for e-commerce. But like anything else and has its disadvantages and advantages.

For most people, advantages far outweigh the disadvantages, but to be fair, both sides should be presented so that you can choose whether or not Shopify is right for your e-commerce venture.

Let's start with some of the advantages of Shopify:

## Advantages Of Shopify

❖ Shopify is competitively priced. The prices that they charge for various packages are comparable with other shopping platforms.

❖ Shopify is extremely easy to use. The backend is modelled after WordPress and so it has much the same look and feel. You can easily figure out how to add products, how to enable or disable features of your store, how to set up payment options and many other useful features. This is probably one of the main strengths of Shopify.

* You can customize the look of your Shopify site using the free themes that come with your membership. This is useful because not every e-commerce platform offers that to you.

* Shopify takes care of a lot of details if you choose to take advantage of their platforms. For example, Shopify has payment gateways already integrated into the backend that you can set up on your store. Shopify also has shipping options available, to make it easy for you to print a label and ship.

* Shopify has a lot of help information in an app store to allow you to add even more features to your site. Some e-commerce platforms have a very noticeable lack of documentation, but Shopify is not one of those. They have a manual that is extremely comprehensive plus additional documentation and live support.

## Disadvantages Of Shopify

The only real disadvantage that Shopify has is an e-commerce platform is the pricing, which was included as an advantage.

The reason that it is also included here is simply because there are e-commerce platforms out there that charge nothing and with Shopify you do end up paying credit card processing fees, app fees, and of course the monthly fee which can range between $29 and $179 a month.

However, for the functionality that you get, the price is still extremely fair. With the $29 a month store and even with paying credit card processing fees you will still have the potential to make a profit with your Shopify store.

## Things to Consider Before Starting a Shopify Store

Before you sign up for your free trial or choose a Shopify plan you are going to want to do some preplanning.

As the axiom goes: if you do not have a destination in mind you have very little chance of arriving there, which means that unless you plan out your store beforehand you are probably not going to be able to laser target it to a niche like you want. The way that you start planning is by asking yourself some questions like these:

# Questions To Help Plan Your Shopify Niche Store

❖ Do you plan on selling real-world products, digital products, or services? Is your pricing based upon a purchase model or a subscription model?

❖ What is your niche going to be? Do you have enough products within that niche to fill a store? Do you have the budget to buy enough inventory to be assured of appealing to enough people? (Obviously, if you are drop shipping this may not be applicable)

❖ What basic store design are you looking for?

❖ How are you planning on fulfilling your orders? Are you going to use Shopify's printing labels, your own fulfilment method or are you using a drop shipper?

❖ What forms of payment are you going to offer? Are you going to use the Shopify included payment gateways or set up something on your own?

## Real-World, Digital or Services and Subscription Models

Nearly every Shopify store out there sells real-world, physical products, but that does not mean you are restricted to physical products.

You could choose to sell eBooks or other digital products, or you could even offer subscription-based services through your Shopify store, to allow access to a specific program or "member's area" of your site.

## Niche Planning

You obviously want to make sure that you can get items that you are going to be selling, and whether or not you can buy those items at a low enough price to be able to mark them up is a part of that. Some store owners even take out a business loan to ensure they have enough inventory to fulfil orders.

## Store Design

The store design that you want is also a planning consideration because you will need to choose between existing Shopify themes, free or premium, or having a web designer create a custom theme for you.

## Order Fulfilment

Shopify has a great system for order fulfilment. You purchase shipping labels from them with postage included and the higher the Shopify package you choose, the more you save. However, there are other shipping methods that you could set up and integrate into your store if you do not want to use Shopify's labels.

## Payment Methods

Shopify has several different payment gateways or methods that you can use. If you want to use their own internal credit card machine, the fees are low, and you will receive payment regularly from Shopify.

They also allow you to set up your own credit card gateway such as using Stripe or to integrate a PayPal payment gateway into your site as well as other forms of currency like Bitcoin and Payza.

# Chapter 1

# How to Choose a Shopify Theme

**S**o, you are wondering how you choose a Shopify theme.

There are a lot of them to choose from and there are a few selection options that you have. Shopify has over 100 free themes in their theme store.

But they also have a large number of premium themes. If you choose a free theme you can install it on your site without incurring an extra charge. The premium themes vary in price usually between $100 and $200, but they can certainly be higher than that.

However, those are not the only two options that you have when it comes to premade themes for Shopify.

# Shopify Options You Might Not Be Aware Of

If you look at the Shopify site, you get the impression that the only place that you can get Shopify themes is actually on the Shopify site. However, that is not the case at all. You can actually find premade Shopify themes all over the web if you type the search term into Google.

There are even more free themes out there that are on the Shopify site, although most of the ones that are on third-party sites do cost money.

## Customizing a Shopify Theme

There are also designers out there that will customize a Shopify theme for you. In fact, there designers out there that will create an entire new Shopify theme for you.

Of course, this is the most expensive of all the options that you have but it will ensure that you get exactly the store that you want. If you have a free or premium theme that you like except for a few small items, you might be able to get a designer to fix those problems for a lot less than you would have to pay someone to design an entire custom theme.

## How To Choose

Which theme you choose will depend on several factors. If you can find a free Shopify theme that fits your stores personality and has all of the functionality and features that you want, go with it. The next step up if you cannot find what you are looking for is to look through the premium themes both on the Shopify site and off.

From there, you are left with getting a designer to customize the theme for you or getting them to change a theme for you. If you have a smaller budget, you might be stuck doing without some features that you want.

## An Overview Of The Shopify App Store

Not everyone knows this, but when you sign up for Shopify you actually get access to a huge number of apps that can integrate with your Shopify site and allow you to have more functionality, more flexibility and add some pretty cool features that might just be the difference between a few sales and a whole lot.

If you are a Shopify store owner, and you have not had the opportunity to visit the App Store yet, here is an overview so you can know what you are going to get, and some good advice about how, why and when you should get apps.

The first thing you should know about the Shopify App Store is that it is not something that included with your Shopify membership. In other words, it has more in common with the themes page. There are free apps that are in the Shopify App Store but most of them are premium, paid apps.

Of course, as always, you get what you pay for, so the free apps may not even be worth your time. However, some of the low-priced apps are really reasonable and have a lot of functionality built in. You would be surprised how many things you can do with Shopify apps.

Shopify can be compared to WordPress as far as the look and feel of the backing goes. If you were to compare Shopify apps to WordPress, they would be equivalent of the WordPress plug-ins. Shopify apps can help you manage your SEO as well as do useful things like allow you to add images for your product variations.

Basically, anything that the Shopify store does not have integrated into it, there is usually an app for it. Before you buy any apps, you definitely should look at the free ones just to make sure that the functionality that you want is an out there. As more and more people develop these apps, the quality of the free apps will likely rise, just like WordPress.

So now you know a little bit more about the Shopify App Store. The apps can definitely add some functionality to your website, and it can be worth investing in a good app that is increasing your sales.

However, try to avoid apps that have a subscription fee rather than a one-time purchase. There are not many of these out there but if you use one, try to find a replacement as soon as you know the app is useful for you.

## Making the Most Use of Shopify

Shopify is one of the most useful platforms in existence because it makes it so easy to set up a store. In order to see just how useful, the program is you have to look at just how difficult it is to set up an ecommerce website.

Here are some of the ways that Shopify has changed the way that people start businesses online:

## You Need To Design a Website

Perhaps you know a web designer that would be willing to design a website for you on the cheap, or even free.

Even if that is the case, you are probably going to have to find a programmer as well because the design elements need to be combined with code in order to make the site functional and allow you to upload products, have a checkout system and for each and every feature that your site requires, you are going to have pay your coder for the hours that he or she spends creating it.

The design and coding come together to build a site and companies often spend tens of thousands of dollars to get the perfect ecommerce website built.

Shopify takes all of the design and programming out of the equation and allows you to choose a unique theme and configure your features from an easy-to-use backend.

## You Need To Incorporate and Secure Payment Gateways

Receiving someone's credit card information is a huge responsibility and stores are required to set up secure payment gateways that make it nearly impossible for hackers to get the payment information.

If you were to set up payment gateways and shopping carts on your site you would need to program all of that security, not to mention automatic shipping calculation, various other checkout features. But Shopify is 100% secure, and you can enable or disable a payment gateway with the click of a button.

## You Need to Fulfil Orders

Imagine if you had to fulfil orders without Shopify. You would have to print out generic shipping labels using third-party software or have your programmer create a shipping label creator.

If you were using a drop shipper, you would have to incorporate their details into your website so that they could receive the customer's information when an order comes through. Setting up order fulfilment on your own is a huge headache and few people want to deal with it, but Shopify makes it simple and easy to do.

## Shopify Takes Care of a Million Details

Shopify takes care of so many things for you that it is almost foolish to try to build an ecommerce site on your own.

From design, security, programming, the third-party application integration to optimizing and making websites responsible for mobile, Shopify has it handled for you.

Shopify is so useful because it takes all of the work out of starting an ecommerce site and allows you to focus on what is truly important – the products that you are selling and the customers that you are selling them to.

# Chapter 2

# Ideas for Selling Physical Products on a Subscription Basis

When you hear the word 'subscription' you will often think of a magazine or perhaps a subscription site.

In other words, you tend to think of this as being an informational product. But what if you have a physical product? Maybe you even have a physical store from which to sell it?

In this case, there are still plenty of great ways to set up a recurring payment scheme and thereby enjoy a much more stable and much more passive income.

Here are some examples of ways you can use this system with a physical product:

## Disposables

If you sell anything from your website that you would describe as being disposable, then a subscription can be a perfect way to sell.

Great examples include food items that might run out quickly, face creams or supplements such as protein shakes.

In all these cases, your buyers can ensure that they get a new product each time they run out and thus never have to worry about running out again!

## Packages

There are many types of physical product that lend themselves well to being sold in a package, this can be another opportunity to provide a useful service by selling a subscription.

A popular example of this for instance is to sell clothes in packs that provide a ready-made outfit.

Several diets have recently become popular by providing the ingredients for meals in a box that is ready to make and eat and that is calorie controlled.

You do not even have to produce these products yourself. This is a great way to sell packages as a reseller for instance – and that way there is no risk because you received the payment in advance!

**Gifts**

If your customers are the forgetful types, then why not let them set up a yearly payment for a gift? This way they can send flowers, chocolates, or jewellery every year on their anniversary for instance!

## Some Tips for Getting More Members on Your Membership Site

If you are monetizing your website by selling a membership, then the main objective of the free content you create is now going to be to convert your visitors into paying subscribers.

This can be a highly lucrative business model and a great way to gain passive, recurring income. At the same time though, convincing people to pay for your content can be difficult. As a rule, most content we discover online is free and as such a lot of us are not used to paying for it.

If you want to make more money from your site, you are going to need to think about how you are going to cross that barrier and get people to put down money for content.

Here are a few tips:

## Make It Sound Exciting

People love to be part of a movement and part of a community. This is how you need to make it sound to be a member of your site - explain to people they will be part of something exciting and be sure to refer to your members as 'VIPs' or 'exclusive members'.

## Offer Levels of Membership

If you want to charge a lot for membership, this can be a difficult challenge to overcome. One useful strategy then is to offer different levels of membership.

Perhaps you charge $5 a month for access to certain pages, but $20 for full, unrestricted access.

## Free Trial

The best way to get someone to buy a puppy is to let them take it home for a week.

You can do something similar with your membership – let your users try it for free so that they see the full benefits and become big fans of what you do. Only ask for payment once your visitors have seen that it is worthwhile!

## Recurring Passive Income Is the Ideal Business Model

A lot of people think that making money online is the perfect set up. In the perfect world, this means earning from a passive income model so that they can even be asleep and still be earning money.

Even when you are working, if you are online then you will be able to make money from the comfort of your home or even while you are sitting on the beach soaking up sun.

But while this is all true, it is also true that working online can be hard work. Even with a passive income, there can never be any guarantee that you are going to have a consistent cash flow. Look at how many businesses were completely destroyed by the Google Panda and Pigeon algorithm changes.

There is one much more reliable form of income for an online business though: and that is recurring income.

## What Is Passive Recurring Income?

Most recurring incomes are still passive. That means they still do not involve trading your time for cash and you can make money even while you are asleep.

At the same time though, these business models remove the possibility of you going a month and not earning anything. That is because you are setting up a recurring fee with your customers/visitors where they have agreed to pay out each month in exchange for your products and services.

For instance, this might mean that you set up a membership website and that in turn will mean that you are charging for your visitors to get access to exclusive content behind a pay wall.

You keep blogging as you normally would, but you can know for a fact that you will have income coming in each month.

Or maybe you create an online course that has a monthly membership, or a web app?

Either way, your money now not only comes in without you having to trade time for cash – but it also comes in on a recurring and reliable basis. It is the ideal business model!

# Chapter 3

# Profiting from Any eCommerce Store

There is a very thin line between success and failure when to comes to any online business.

That is to say, that if you have a good business model but it is not making you a lot of money right now, it could be the tiniest thing that is currently holding you back.

Likewise, it might be that the smallest little change could take your currently struggling business model and turn it into a massive money maker.

One example of just such a small change that can make all the difference, is to add at least one very cheap item to your ecommerce store.

Whether you are making money from subscriptions or one-off payments, this can make a massive difference.

## Why a Cheap Item Can Make a Massive Difference

The problem when trying to sell a 'big ticket' item on an online store, is that you are basically trying to overcome two very powerful 'barriers' to making a sale.

The first and most obvious barrier is that your product is expensive, and people take a lot of convincing if they are going to buy something for a lot of money.

The second barrier is that people do not like buying online from new sources. If they have never dealt with your business before, then they will be concerned about security and they will not know whether to trust your delivery system.

Thus, trying to get someone to pay for something very expensive on a completely alien site is an up-hill battle.

On the other hand, though, if you can get them to buy one very small item – even if it just costs $5 – this will now make it much easier to get them to buy future items for much more money.

Especially if you provide them with a great service and a really high-quality product!

## Increasing Ecommerce Your Sales

If you have an ecommerce store of any kind, then whether you are selling a digital product, a physical product or a subscription, there are a few techniques you can employ to make even more sales. And it is all about the way you set up your store...

### Use a Red 'Buy Now' Button

If you make your buy now button red, research shows that it will get more clicks than if you were to make it any other colour.

### Make Multiple Bundles at Different Price Points

One of the best ways to sell more products is to give your customers more control over the way they want to buy them. If you create multiple 'bundles' for instance, this might mean that you let your customers buy more items at once and make bigger savings or choose to buy just a few individual items from your larger batch and thereby spend less money in total.

Either way, you can help your customers feel as though they are saving money or making a savvy decision while still buying from you!

## Sell Some Very Cheap Items

If you are trying to sell a very expensive product from your ecommerce store, then this means you are essentially trying to accomplish two very difficult things. The first difficult thing is trying to get your customers to part with a lot of cash and to buy something big.

The second? You are trying to earn their trust and get them to spend money with you when they have never dealt with your service before.

Do not try and do both these things at once! Sell a cheap item and that way you can build trust – then you can move onto more expensive items later.

## Offer Free Samples

Better yet why not offer a free sample?

If you sell a membership site then you can offer a free membership with reduced features or you can offer a free, full membership for a limited period.

# Chapter 4

# Using Affiliates to Sell More

**A**dding affiliate programs to your ecommerce store is a fantastic way to greatly increase the sales you make.

Generally, the term affiliate tends to be associated with one-off payments for digital products, informational products. In fact, though, there is no reason for this to be the case...

## What Is an Affiliate Program?

An affiliate program is essentially a strategy that can be used by online marketers to increase their sales. In essence, you will be offering other marketers commission for helping you to sell your products. This commission can be as much as you like – whether it is 10% or 75% - but the more you offer the more affiliate marketers you will attract.

What this then means is that you now have additional people helping you to promote and sell your products. Of course, this is on top of what you were already selling – so that means you will not lose any of the income you already have, you will just gain even more additional income.

In theory, this can then help you to attract any number of affiliates. And if it works out, that now means you will have a legion of professional marketers with huge audiences helping you to sell your product. Imagine if you managed to get ten affiliates and each one helped you to sell an additional twenty products a month?

Better yet, even the affiliates that do not land you direct sales will still be getting more exposure for your product and for your brand!

## How to Set Up Affiliate Programs

Setting up and affiliate program is actually very easy and straightforward too.

All you need to do is to set up your Shopify account as normal and then add an app that is designed to provide affiliate options. That is the great thing about Shopify – it is endlessly expandable!

## Using Content Marketing for Your Shopify Store

If you are looking for a way to make money as a blogger, then one of the simplest possible options is to take your current strategy, add some more content marketing and then use Shopify to turn it into a membership site.

### What Is Content Marketing?

Content marketing means marketing a website or blog by adding lots of content to it. This then makes it easier for people to find you on Google and it lets people share content they enjoy on your site.

But more than this, it also allows you to build trust and authority with your audience and thereby to make more sales. The idea is simple: someone finds your content through Google and reads a blog post or article you have written.

In doing so, they learn something interesting, and they are thoroughly entertained. Thus, they look out for your logo in future. Eventually, your visitors decide they want to bookmark your page or subscribe to your RSS feed because they really enjoy what you are putting out.

Then they see that you have extra content that is premium and that costs them money. You manage to make it very clear that behind that paywall is your very best stuff that can really benefit them.

Finally, the make the plunge and decide to sign up for your content.

You can even make this easier for them by providing a free trial membership, or by making it very easy for them to cancel. Either way, you will now have a perfect means of converting first time visitors into long-term readers and eventually paying customers.

And because that payment is a recurring payment, this means it is perfectly predictable and 100% reliable. You have right here a very simple and easy method for securing a lot of money for the long-term future!

# Chapter 5

# Getting Stock Photos for Your Shopify Store

**I**f you are selling items online that you do not actually physically have at your location or if you have the items at your location but you just do not have the facilities to take good photos you might want to consider using stock photos for the products in your Shopify store.

There are actually quite a few companies out there that deal with product stock photos and you may be able to find what you are looking for. If you are selling specialized products that do not have stock photos you may have to consider other options which will discuss here.

# Where to Find Stock Photos Of Products

Many people that set up an online store get their product images directly from a Google image search. However, this can be a very bad idea.

If you have taken an image that a competitor of yours actually took themselves and then placed on their website, you may run afoul of intellectual property law. If someone takes a photograph, the rights to it are usually theirs.

However, that does not mean that all is lost. You may politely ask the retailer where they get their images and see if there is some way that you can get access to the same images.

## Stock Photo Websites

Do not waste a lot of time looking on stock photo websites for your product photos. Do a quick Google search and see if any of the first few results are from a stock photo image. If not, you probably are going to find that particular product on any stock photo page.

A lot of the time, what stock photo websites have, are images of a particular product model that represents all of the products in that category.

For example, they may have a picture of a specific blender model, but they are not listing it is the model they are simply listing it as a blender.

## Ask the Manufacturer

One of the things that you can do that many storeowners do not even think about is contact the manufacturer and get suggestions from them as to where you can get photos of the products that you are selling.

Some manufacturers even have stock photos that they have taken for various marketing purposes but even if they do not, they will probably be able to point you in the right direction so that you can find a viable source.

## Using Pinterest To Make Sales In Your Shopify Store

If you own a Shopify store, odds are that you already know about the social media tie-ins that you can do, especially adding the buy button to Pinterest posts.

However, even though this is available, and everyone knows that social media can be a valuable source of sales, there are still people out there that resist using Pinterest – mostly because they have never used it and are a little uneasy about a new social media platform, particularly one that uses pictures as its primary form of communication and not words.

So, if you are not currently using Pinterest with your Shopify store, here are four tips that will help you use this social media powerhouse to make sales.

Use Coupons: Pinterest users love coupons, and they love the exclusivity that comes from discovering something on Pinterest and then being able to save money on it.

You can use third-party sites like Groupon to set up deals, as well as applications like Wishpond.

Then, you can create a coupon board on your Pinterest page that people can check often.

Do not neglect SEO: Many people use Pinterest for their business with no regard to optimizing their Pinterest page, pins, or boards for search engines. Always use good SEO practices with Pinterest.

Run contests: If you want to make your Pinterest follows take note and increase the traffic to your Shopify store then you want to run contests regularly. Contests are exciting and they end up being shared a lot more often.

Contests can introduce you to a whole new audience on Pinterest. You can either host the coupons on your own Shopify site or you can host them on Pinterest and drive traffic to your site and the previous application mentioned – Wishpond – also works well for contests.

Use rich pins: Rich pins are something relatively new to Pinterest. Rich pins allow you to pin recipe pins, movie pins and pins on a specific product, which is what you want.

You are allowed to update price, product availability and more, plus there is more content for the search engines to find, which means more traffic.

Rich pins can be used to showcase special products that you are currently trying to promote, or you can use them for your products whenever you post them. This will allow you to get traffic to Pinterest and send it straight to your store.

# Chapter 6

# How Shopify Pays Store Owners

**I**f you are considering Shopify one of the things that you are going to want to know is how you are going to get paid.

Shopify has a built-in payment gateway that uses their credit card machines to process all of your sales. At regular intervals, Shopify pays the storeowners what they are owed, minus any credit card fees that come with your Shopify plan.

This is actually a really great way to accept payments because it is 100% secure, already integrated into your Shopify site and very easy to use. But you might be wondering how you get paid. Here is the lowdown on how Shopify pays their storeowners.

## Shopify Funds Transfer

So, how to Shopify actually pay you? The fact is, you will be able to set that up yourself and your site's admin area. You can have your money in as little as three days if you live in the United States or Australia. If you live in Canada or the United Kingdom you have to wait seven days. Remember, those are business days not days of the week.

For banks, business days are Monday, Tuesday, Wednesday, Thursday, and Friday only, as long as they are not on federal holidays when they are closed.

However, that does not mean that Shopify works by the same rules that banks do. Shopify will transfer your funds every day. So, you might see that it is paid in your account, but you actually have not gotten a payment yet.

That means, most likely, the deposit has been sent out, but your bank has not actually processed it and put it into your account. It could be the same day that you see it says paid or it could be the very next day depending on the processing speed of your bank.

Some of the other things that you need to keep in mind is that your first payment probably is not going to happen soon.

Shopify wants to make sure that there is no fraud going on with all of their new members and so they take the time to carefully check whenever somebody has a first-time payment.

It is usually only a few extra days. Also bear in mind, that for some products, Shopify is required to pay only every 30 days. Finally, you will also have the occasional refund to deal with. Shopify deposits refunds immediately after issue, but it could take a few days to get your customers bank account or credit card.

## How Does Shopify Support Work?

If you Shopify store or you are considering a Shopify store, you might be wondering what sort of support options are available to you and how they actually work. You will be pleased to know that Shopify's customer support is one of the reasons that the platform is so popular. In this chapter, we will explore that popularity as it relates to the customer service that Shopify offers its merchants.

If you are considering going with Shopify this will allow you to evaluate their customer service and determine whether or not you want to work with the platform.

Shopify has four basic support functions. The first one that we will talk about is the documentation. There is a lot of documentation that comes with Shopify.

There is a comprehensive manual that covers every single thing that you need to know to set up a Shopify store. It is a little difficult to navigate and find exactly what you are looking for, but it certainly is comprehensive.

Shopify also has their e-commerce University in their member forums which can help your advice from other people that have stores on Shopify.

The second support type that will discuss is email. You can find the email contact form by clicking on the support link from any documentation page and then scrolling down so that you can see the three support options. You can use email anytime to contact Shopify but there are two other options that you can use if you need help right away.

One of those options is live chat. Live chat is available from the Shopify experts 24 hours a day, 365 days a year. The great thing with the live chat is that you can instantly connect with someone who can help you and they will be able to look over your store to see where you are having a problem.

The live chat support operators are knowledgeable and helpful, and many people rate Shopify's customer service is so high because of them.

Finally, you have the ability to call Shopify at any time. Shopify has toll-free numbers for the United States, United Kingdom, Australia, New Zealand, and Singapore. This is also a 24-hour, 365-day service that you can get a hold of quickly and get help for whatever problem that you are experiencing.

This is definitely a bonus because if you are having a problem with your site you may be losing money with every hour that it is down.

# Chapter 7

# Brick-and-Mortar Store Work Hand-in-Hand with Shopify

**I** **f you have a brick-and-mortar store, and you are thinking about opening an online store using Shopify, you might be wondering just how that would work and whether or not the two are compatible.**

Rest assured, their business owners all over the world the do exactly that. In fact, because of the economy, business owners are struggling everywhere.

Many of them adopt their e-commerce website in the hopes that their business will be profitable once again. Here are some things to keep in mind if you already have a brick-and-mortar store.

## Let Your Real-World Customers Know

You definitely want to let the customers that come into your store know that you have an e-commerce website with your products. This means that if they are at home and are thinking about visiting your store, they can just look online and see if you have the product that they want.

That is a much easier task than going all the way to your store or even calling to find out if you have what they are looking for.

What you are basically doing is offering your customers an instant way to look up a product that they want, but it also means that you are actually going to have to list those products on your website.

## Offer Free In-Store Pickup

Another way that this can be very beneficial for your brick-and-mortar store is to allow your customers to buy online and then come into your store to pick it up. This is become a very popular practice for customers of Walmart who have embraced the option so enthusiastically that they have had to set up a separate department in their stores just to deal with people that bought online and came in to pick up their items.

Your customers may appreciate being able to buy online and pick up their merchandise at their leisure.

## Never Miss an Opportunity To Advertise

You never know when an online customer is going to be able to influence our real-world customer or the other way around. Make sure that you are not only sharing your web address with your real-world customers and advertising your website through other channels in your local area, but that you are also advertising your brick-and-mortar store to your online customers.

One example of when this works out well is when an online customer has a relative or friend in your area.

## How Do Taxes Work On Shopify

So, you are a new Shopify store owner. You might be wondering about taxes. Anytime someone sells products online they have to worry about sales tax. But not everyone pays sales tax, and you may not have to pay tax on any of the orders that you sell.

In addition, you have to worry about income tax. If you have worked for yourself before you know that as an independent contractor or self-employed individual you have to pay your own taxes and that means keeping track of things like expenses, income and other factors.

## Sales Tax

So how does sales-tax work? It actually differs from one state to another in the United States. If you are outside of the United States, you will have an entirely different set of tax laws to deal with.

However, a good rule of thumb to go by is that if you sell a product in the state or province that you are currently located in and the buyer is also in your state or province, you will have to pay taxes on it. Obviously, the state sales tax rate where you live will be applicable.

One of the things that you want to keep in mind is that you should set aside your sales tax right away because the state is going to want you to pay your sales tax every three months or so.

If you do not have it when it comes due, you could be stuck with some pretty hefty fines and your business to be closed down after repeated violations.

Besides having to pay sales tax on any products that you sell within your own state, you are also going to have to pay your own income tax. This is only payable once per year at the same time that you normally would file your taxes if you had a regular job.

If you have not been self-employed before, it is both a blessing and a curse. You might be able to pay less tax than you normally would, because of your expenses, but you also have to set a pretty big chunk of money aside from all of your income to make sure that you can cover your tax since you will not know how much a low until the very end of the year.

Of course, once you figure out what you owe and you write the check, you will have an instant tax return.

## Setting Up Product Variants With Shopify

If you have a Shopify store the sales real-world items one of the things that you may have to deal with is product variants. Luckily, Shopify handles this very well, unlike some of the e-commerce platforms that are out there.

This chapter will demonstrate how you can use Shopify to do product variants but before that, let's discuss what a product variant actually is.

Product variants are the different types of product that you have in your store. Let's take a shirt for example: you have several different sizes with this particular shirt such as small, medium, large and XL.

Then you may have several different colours as well. For example, this particular shirt may come in blue, red, green, black and gray. You might have a third variant as well; this shirt comes in both a regular T-shirt style with a rounded collar and a V-neck collar.

In order to offer this product in your store you are going to want to set up these product variants on the same listing.

You do not want to make separate listings for all of these different products because the different listings may number in the hundreds for one thing, and this is a lot of extra work, but mostly, it is because you do not want your customers to have to search your entire site to find the size that they want or the style.

# How To Set Up Product Variants

Here are the steps that you will go through if you are trying to create product variants through the Shopify admin panel. First, go to your admin area and go to the pricing, inventory, and shipping section. There will be a link there to allow you to add variants for whichever product it is.

You will create two things to make your variants. The first is the option name, which in the case of our example would be colour, size, and style.

For each of these, you are going to set your option values, which are the different sizes and colours that we discussed earlier.

You are able to set a different price in a different barcode for each variant and customize the listing the way you need to.

After you have your variants added to your products you want to make sure that you optimize for the search engines for your variant products as much as you possibly can. In case someone is looking for a product that you sell in a specific colour try to ensure that it will appear in the search engines.

# Chapter 8

# Growing Your Ecommerce Business

So, how do you grow your ecommerce business so that instead of a trickle of sales coming in regularly you get a flood of sales that will allow you to change your life and run your store full-time?

There is no one tried-and-true method, obviously; otherwise, everyone with a small ecommerce store would succeed. It takes a small amount of luck but a much larger amount of hard work and no matter how much luck you do have, these tips on growing your business to epic proportions will definitely work for you.

## Continually Build on Your SEO and Keep Up With The Latest Trends

You are looking at the big picture so if you are posting blog entries on your site, make sure they are of the highest quality. If you are getting links for content posted elsewhere, make sure that they are going to stand the test of time. Whatever SEO techniques you are using, make sure that they will still be able to boost your site in the future.

This includes being very careful about which SEO companies you choose to work with. Make sure that you know all of the methods that they are using and that they are all white-hat and intended to be long-term.

## Look for Viral Opportunities

A good marketer will begin to get a second sense for viral opportunities when they come and if you can figure out what the trends are going to be and jump on them when you do figure it out.

Of course, this is often more down to chance than anything else, but all it could take is one time being viral to see your store start to grow quickly, especially if you are doing all of the other things that you should be doing.

## Always Be Evolving

This is probably the most important advice that you can take to heart regarding your ecommerce website. Pay attention to what is going on and continue to evolve and be prepared for the future. When the shift to mobile devices happened, the companies that were adopting early were the most successful ones on mobile even after everyone else started optimizing.

When the next shift happens, you want to make sure that you know it is going to happen and that your store is able to start implementing changes that will give you success long-term. Changes are going to happen, and if you are ready, you can be very successful.

## Marketing Your Shopify Website

Once you have your website designed, your products uploaded, your site tested and working, you will need to do some marketing. You are not going to get very many visitors if you do not get your name out there. There are dozens of ways that you can market your Shopify site and get some sales with your efforts, but we are going to discuss three methods here.

## Social Media Marketing

Shopify is ready-made for social media marketing. They have worked very hard to incorporate your social media into your store so that you can sell to those who are following you on your networks.

This is important for many business owners because they have a significant following on social media websites, and they are expecting to be able to advertise to those followers.

In fact, for many, their business plan depends upon it. Shopify allows you not only to integrate social media into your Shopify site so that people can find you there, but they also allow you to use 'Buy' buttons on your social media posts.

Some of the most useful tools that are provided by Shopify when you have a store with them is the integration of the buy button on Pinterest.

Pinterest has become one of the most successful ways that store owners can market their products, because all you have to do is post a photo of a great item and watch the referrals roll in.

However, Pinterest is not the only social media site that offers this integration. You also get buy buttons on Twitter and Facebook to make your social media platforms a place to find new customers and fans.

## Great Customer Service

The second way that you can ensure that your store is going to grow is by always providing great customer service. Take Amazon as your example. They have some of the best customer service on the market today and people go back to them because of how well they are treated with something goes wrong.

If you want your customers to remember you and continue to buy from you, then offer them great customer service, because it is a rarity today and you will definitely stand out. It can be difficult to handle each customer's problem quickly, completely when you are a one-person operation, but it will be vital later on, so you might want to think about hiring a customer service rep if you can afford it.

## Build Expertise

The more of an expert you become in the field, the more people are going to want to buy from you. If you are an expert on sports equipment, people will come to you to ask questions about it, advice on what to buy and more importantly, they will follow your recommendations.

That means that when you list an items in your store, they are going to be motivated to buy simply because it is in a store that they see as one of the leading experts on the topic.

# Chapter 9

# Building a Brand That People Will Want to Buy From

**N**o matter what type of product you intend on selling online and whether or not that product is something you created yourself, it is always crucial that you have a strong brand in order to encourage sales.

The aim is not only to get people to want to buy a particular product but also to get them to want to buy that product from you. Why would they come to your site to buy their fitness clothing when they can buy the exact same thing from Amazon?

How do you build the trust and familiarity that makes people want to buy from you?

## What Is a Brand?

It starts by understanding precisely what a brand is – and what it is not. A brand is much more than just a logo and a company name. Instead, your brand is the mission statement that holds your company together and drives you forward. It is the answer to the question: 'Why do you do what you do?'

This is what a lot of businesses completely misunderstand and that in turn is what prevents them from fulfilling their full potential. If the only objective of your brand is to sell products, then it will be uninspiring and uninteresting, and no one will have any particular affiliation with you or interest in buying from you over another seller.

We have all been to sites like that: they are bland, plain, and completely devoid of passion. But now think of the brands that you actually love.

They will have a driving motivation behind them and an ethos that you agree with.

Perhaps you like an organic food brand that seems to really care about improving the health of its customers and avoiding anything that will damage their health. Perhaps they want to make the world a cleaner and eco-friendlier place. And that makes you want to shop with them.

It makes you excited to try out their product recommendations. Perhaps the brand you love is a weight training brand that is all about pushing yourself harder and that is all about grit and determination. If that speaks to you, then you will want to wear that logo!

## Communicating Your Brand

But it is one thing to have a real mission statement and passion behind your brand – it is another thing entirely to communicate that with your audience and to get them to believe you.

So how do you go about doing this and making sure that people really understand what you are all about?

A good start is to have a logo and a company name that perfectly explains who you are and what you do. This should be designed specifically for a particular target audience. That is to say that you should never try to cater to everyone but rather to cater strongly to a particular person.

The aim is that if someone sees just one of your products or blog posts, combined with your company name and your logo... that alone should be enough to tell them that they will love your brand and will want to follow it!

## Pricing and Positioning Your Items to Increase Sales

What determines how well an item sells? Many people think it is the quality of the item. Others think it is the quality of the marketing. But actually, it is both those things and lots more. The rather daunting aspect of selling a product is that you need to get everything right and that countless tiny factors are all influencing how well your product sells (or does not) at any given time.

This is good news too though, as it means that at any point, you can probably encourage more sales by tweaking your approach in one area or another. For example: even changing the way you arrange your items in an ecommerce store can make a big difference to how they sell!

## Using Contrast

Contrast is an interesting concept in retail that suggests you should place two items next to each other that have contrasting price points. In other words, place your expensive ties right next to your cheap ties. Why is this? Because it makes both items look better. For the expensive ties, being next to the cheaper ties makes them seem more luxurious and premium.

What is more, is that if someone were thinking that they were going to buy the cheap ties, they might notice that the expensive ones are there and that for just a little more money, they could have the very most luxurious line that you stock. They might not initially have been interested in buying a tie for $50. But seeing as it is only $15 more expensive than the cheap ties, why not bump up the expense and get the very best?

Conversely, this now makes the cheap tie seem like an even better bargain. And if your customer is debating whether or not they should make a purchase, they can use this as a way to convince themselves. 'Well,' they might think, 'at least if I just buy the cheap tie, I will have saved myself some money!'.

## Selling One Cheap Item

Something I always recommend is that an ecommerce store sell at least one very cheap item. This is important because when someone shops with you for the first time, they might not fully trust your service or even how secure your payments are. Thus, they will not want to spend a large amount of money and risk it not showing up!

But by selling one item very cheaply, you can convince someone to take a risk when there is not that much money at stake. This way, they can see that you provide a reliable service and hopefully they will then be happy to use your business in future for more expensive products!

There are many more strategies like these that you can use to sell products, and these vary from bundling products together, to offering limited-time discounts in order to drive sales.

Ultimately though, the take home lesson is that if you want something to sell faster, you might want to think about the way you are presenting it in your ecommerce store.

# Conclusion

**If you are selling products through a dropshipping business on Shopify or if you are selling a digital product as an affiliate, then it is absolutely crucial that you build a relationship with your potential customers before you try and sell to them.**

This is something that a lot of sellers and marketers just do not understand and ultimately it is to their detriment as they end up missing out on the opportunity to sell. Read on to see exactly what this means and why it is so important...

An analogy... The best way to explain this is with an analogy, or two. Imagine for a moment that you see an attractive lady or man at a bar, and you want to get to know them a little better.

So, what you do, is you go up and you ask if they are come home with you tonight. What do you think happens next? Most likely you get a firm slap in the face – and this is more than fair enough!

The problem with this approach is that the person does not know you yet. They do not know what you are like and if they are likely to have a good time with you and more importantly – they do not know if they can trust you! You might be dangerous as far as they are concerned!

Another scenario is someone trying to sell a watch. Imagine they come up to you in the street holding a watch and ask if you want to buy it for $2,000. What do you say? Again, you will probably turn and run.

No one would spend that much money on something without knowing anything about it and without having any form of 'come back' in case the deal turns sour.

# How Businesses Make This Mistake All the Time

Both these examples probably seem absurd to you, but this is essentially what many businesses are doing all the time. If you have a website that tries to sell a product as soon as anyone lands on it, then you are going to drive people away before they have even had a chance to read your site.

They may well be interested in what you are selling but if they do not know your brand and they do not know your product, then they will not want to buy right away. And if all you are interested in doing is selling to them with tons of pop-up ads, then you are going to drive them off – it will look like spam!

Now consider the alternative approach: they land on your website and they find tons of great content that is well written, free, and informative. This allows the visitor to form a positive opinion of your business and hopefully to become interested in the products you are mentioning.

And as a result, they are much more likely to want to buy from you in future. So instead of focusing on making a sale, focus on making a fan. Push them toward a mailing list instead and invite them to come back. That way, the sales will come to you!

# Checklist

It is recommended that you print this checklist out so you can work side-by-side with the main eBook.

Idea of this checklist is to mark off 1-by-1 what you've learned and had an understanding about.

Once you have had a full understanding of each chapter, topics, and subject throughout the main eBook, simply check it off. A great way to keep organized and not backtracking what you already have learned.

❖ Introduction

  o What Is Shopify?

  o Features and Benefits

  o Pros and Cons Of The Shopify Platform

    • Advantages Of Shopify

    • Disadvantages Of Shopify

  o Things To Consider Before Starting a Shopify Store

- Questions To Help Plan Your Shopify Niche Store

- Real-World, Digital or Services and Subscription Models

- Niche Planning

- Store Design

- Order Fulfillment

- Payment Methods

❖ How To Choose a Shopify Theme

   o Shopify Options You Might Not Be Aware Of

   - Customizing a Shopify Theme

   - How To Choose

   o An Overview Of The Shopify App Store

   o Making The Most Use Of Shopify

   - You Need To Design a Website

   - You Need To Incorporate and Secure Payment Gateways

   - You Need To Fulfill Orders

- Shopify Takes Care Of a Million Details

❖ Ideas For Selling Physical Products On a Subscription Basis

- o Some Tips For Getting More Members On Your Membership Site

  - Make It Sound Exciting

  - Offer Levels Of Membership

  - Free Trial

- o Recurring Passive Income Is The Ideal Business Model

  - What Is Passive Recurring Income?

❖ Profiting From Any eCommerce Store

- o Why a Cheap Item Can Make a Massive Difference

- o Increasing Ecommerce Your Sales

  - Use a Red 'Buy Now' Button

  - Make Multiple Bundles at Different Price Points

  - Sell Some Very Cheap Items

  - Offer Free Samples

❖ Using Affiliates to Sell More

    o What Is an Affiliate Program?

    o How To Set Up Affiliate Programs

    o Using Content Marketing For Your Shopify Store

        • What Is Content Marketing?

❖ Getting Stock Photos For Your Shopify Store

    o Where To Find Stock Photos Of Products

    o Stock Photo Websites

    o Ask The Manufacturer

    o Using Pinterest To Make Sales In Your Shopify Store

❖ How Shopify Pays Store Owners

    o Shopify Funds Transfer

    o How Does Shopify Support Work?

❖ Brick-and-Mortar Store Work Hand-in-Hand with Shopify

    o Let Your Real-World Customers Know

    o Offer Free In-Store Pickup

- o Never Miss an Opportunity To Advertise

- o How Do Taxes Work On Shopify

  - Sales Tax

  - Income Tax

- o Setting Up Product Variants With Shopify

  - How To Set Up Product Variants

- ❖ Growing Your Ecommerce Business

  - o Continually Build On Your SEO and Keep Up With The Latest Trends

  - o Look For Viral Opportunities

  - o Always Be Evolving

  - o Marketing Your Shopify Website

    - Social Media Marketing

    - Great Customer Service

    - Build Expertise

- ❖ Building a Brand That People Will Want to Buy From

- What Is a Brand?

- Communicating Your Brand

- Pricing and Positioning Your Items To Increase Sales

  - Using Contrast

  - Selling One Cheap Item

# ECOMMERCE

# MASTERY

# Introduction

With advent of systems like Shopify and WooCommerce that make it easier than ever to set up an online store without vast programming knowledge or deep pockets, and the prevalence of drop shipping companies that have affordable prices, e-commerce is booming like never before.

E-commerce is one of the only systems you can use to make money online that is truly long-lasting and sustainable, and, in a profitable niche, can keep making you money for many years to come.

In fact, there are ordinary people with no business background, no advanced education, and no huge starting bank account balances who are making millions selling everyday items. If you are interested in starting your own online store, I recommend reading this guide from start to finish. I will teach you the basics, and it is up to you to pursue it.

So let's get started.

# Choosing a Profitable Niche

You can create the coolest, best looking, most exciting online store ever created, and fail miserably if you do not choose a profitable niche. Niche selection is so important that it can literally make or break your success.

A good niche should:

❖ Have a moderate to large audience

❖ Have low to moderate competition

❖ Have buyers who are passionate about the niche

❖ Have products that are priced high enough to be profitable

You want to make sure there are enough people who are interested in the niche to support a good number of sales, but you do not want the niche to be so saturated that it is difficult to make a profit.

You want a market in which the buyers are passionate or have a real need for the product. It is going to be difficult to make good money selling ordinary products unless you have a very unique selling point, such as a drastically lower price, or some sort of value-added selling point.

You want to sell products people will be excited to buy, and that they will keep coming back for.

You want to make sure you have products that can be priced high enough to make you a good product without pricing you out of the market.

You probably will not make a lot of money selling products priced under a dollar, because you will not be able to build a large enough market quickly enough, but a product priced at ten dollars or more would probably be enough to justify the opening of a store.

Of course, there are people who have made fortunes with very inexpensive products, but it takes more volume than a beginner could likely manage.

A good starting point for niche research is to simply make a list of your own hobbies, interests, areas of knowledge, and needs. The more you know about a particular subject when you open the store, the easier it will be for you to source products people would want to buy and to find the right marketing channels to reach your core audience.

Once you have a list of at least 10-20 topics, you can begin to research them in earnest. You want to find out how many people might be interested in each potential niche, how many products are available that you could sell, and how much of a profit margin would be possible.

There are many different ways to do this, but one of the most popular ways is to check Amazon. Start by searching for individual products you might buy in a particular niche. For example, if you want to research the golf niche, search for things like golf clubs and golf balls and find out the bestseller rank for each product. This will give you a general idea of how well each product sells.

You want to be able to find at least a few products selling well enough to be in the top 10,000 in their main category, and in the top 1,000 would be even better.

Here is an example from a live Amazon listing for a particular brand of gold balls:

This product is currently #857 in its main category (Sports & Outdoors), which shows there is a strong market for golf balls, especially when I Ecom Mastery: Special Report 9 take a look at other products in the Golf Balls category. The top product in this category is #125 in Sports & Outdoors.

Now, you should be aware that strong demand within a main category might not always mean huge sales. Some categories will have fewer sales than others, of course. But this will give you a general idea if there is a market in the niche.

If you want to learn more about niche selection, I highly recommend checking out Ecom Smart Start. You will learn all about niche selection from start to finish, including dozens of broad niche topics you can use as a starting point for your brainstorming.

# Finding Your Passion

It is not enough to choose a niche that is profitable. If you choose a niche you are not passionate about, or one that you find you truly dislike, your business is likely to turn into a drudgery very quickly. In fact, one of the reasons many people start a business is to get away from jobs they hate, and the last thing you want is to end up in the same position you were in before you left your job—unhappy and wanting something different.

So, as you look for potential niches, try to find something that interests you and you are passionate about. This will make it easier for you to source products, market the products, and spend the time required to make your store a success.

It is possible that you will not have any interests that would be profitable, but it is highly unlikely.

Even if you like some relatively obscure things, there will usually be at least a decent number of other people who are also interested in it.

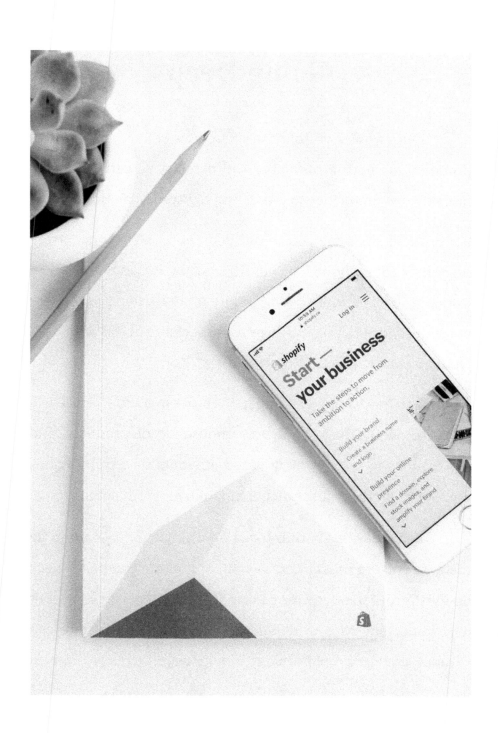

# Going Deep

Once you have found a niche you believe has a lot of potential for both profitability and passion, you should try to drill down even further to create the tightest niche possible.

For example, let's say you've decided you want to concentrate on the outdoor hobby niche. This might include things like camping, backpacking, hiking, hunting, and fishing. But there are thousands of popular stores that specialize in this area, so it would be quite difficult to compete.

In order to have an all-encompassing store in a broad niche like this, you would have to source thousands of products, and make sure the prices stay updated. It would be a tremendous amount of work for just one person, or even a small team.

Instead, it is good to focus on a single area. It could be the area you are most interested in, or the one you believe will be most profitable (as long as you are still interested in it). But it is important to drill down to the tightest niche you can without going so tight that it would be difficult to find an audience or source products.

For example, instead of "outdoor hobbies", you could drill down a bit to fishing. This may still be too broad, so you could drill down to fly fishing.

This is pretty good, but you might even go a little further to specialize in a specific type of fly, or maybe into fly tying supplies for people who want to tie their own flies for fishing.

Keep drilling down until you reach a point when you can no longer find enough products to source or interest in the niche. You would be surprised just how far you can go in many niches! For example, blacksocks.com specializes in—you guessed it— black socks. They also have other products that they expanded into, such as coloured socks and underwear, but they started out selling black socks and have been wildly successful!

# Sourcing Products

There are three main ways you can source products for your ecommerce store:

1. You can use a drop shipper.

2. You can buy through a wholesale company or the manufacturer.

3. You can create the products yourself.

Each method has its own pros and cons, and no single method is the best method for every single store, so let's talk about those factors so you can decide the best way to source products for your store.

# Drop Shipping

In case you are not familiar with drop shipping, the way it works is that you take orders on your store, and once someone orders from you and pays you, you go to the drop shipper's website and order the product. The product is sent directly to the buyer from the drop shipper, and you keep the difference as your profit.

Let's say you are selling a snow globe for $10. The drop shipper charges $5 for that snow globe. Your customer pays you $10, plus whatever shipping cost you charge. Then you go buy the product from the drop shipper for $5 and you keep $5 in profit.

There are also systems you can use that will automate the ordering process for you, such as plugins for major e-commerce platforms like WooCommerce and Shopify.

The major benefit of this method is that you do not have to pay upfront for merchandise, so you can pretty much start your store for free, minus the cost of a domain name, hosting, etc.

Additionally, you do not have to deal with having warehouse space to store the merchandise or dealing with packing and shipping. But the drawback is that you lose a lot of control, which can cause issues at times.

For example, you will not be able to ensure that the correct product is sent to your customer, and you will not be able to control the shipping speed.

# Buying Wholesale

The most common method of sourcing products for most stores, both online and offline, is buying wholesale from the manufacturer or from a wholesaler that acts as a middleman.

You will generally get better prices buying wholesale than from a drop shipper, because most drop shippers are middlemen who must markup wholesale prices to make a profit. This is one of the biggest benefits to this particular method of sourcing.

You will also have more control, because you can be certain you are sending the right product to the customer, and you can control how it is packed and shipped. This results in fewer returns.

However, you will need to have warehouse space to store the products, a system to manage inventory, and time to package and ship all the products to your buyers.

Additionally, many people cannot afford the substantial cash outlay of buying inventory upfront. This is one reason why many online stores start with drop shipping.

# Creating Your Own Products

The final way of sourcing products is to make them yourself. If you have a hobby you love, such as making jewellery or painting, you can create all of your products. You can also create a prototype for a product and search for companies to manufacture the product for you. This can be prohibitively expensive for many, but it is a fantastic way to have a unique product.

There are many benefits to this, such as having a product no one else has, which can increase sales. But there are a few drawbacks, too.

For example, it can be quite expensive to make your own products. If you make them by hand, you still have to purchase materials. If you get a company to produce the products, you run into huge start-up costs.

Having your own unique products will almost always be the best option.

If you can afford it, but you can always build your brand on drop shipping or wholesale products and move into your own stuff later.

# Marketing Your Store

"If you build it, they will come."

You have probably heard that quote before, right? It comes from the 1989 movie Field of Dreams, starting Kevin Costner.

A lot of people seem to live by that mantra, with books, blogs, websites, YouTube channels, online stores... just about anything you can think of in the business world.

But unless you are very lucky, people are not just going to magically find your store and start buying from you. You have to get out there and bring in visitors.

Let's talk about a few cool ways you can market your store as a beginner.

# Have A USP

It is very important that your store have a USP—a Unique Selling Point, or Unique Selling Proposition. This is something that sets your store apart from all, or at least most, of your competition, and gives people a reason to shop with you instead of someone else.

If you are selling a very unique product, that alone is your USP. However, if you are selling something that is available at many other stores, you need something that will set you apart.

Here are a few suggestions:

❖ **Free shipping** – This may or may not be possible based on your profit margins, or you may have to include free shipping only with a purchase over a certain dollar amount, but this is a great way to get people to order from you instead of your competition.

❖ **Specialize** – We talked about the importance of drilling down as far as possible in a niche, and that is because it can really set you apart from the competition. It is a great USP.

❖ **Include bonuses** – People love getting stuff for free. Including bonuses with purchase, even small bonuses, can be a great way to boost customer loyalty, gain repeat purchases, and attract people to your store. Shops that are well known for this include Fingerhut and Baker Creek Heirloom Seeds.

❖ **Create bundles** – Bundles are a great way to set yourself apart from the competition. Let's say you have a shop selling kits for building model cars. You could have a beginner's model building kit that contains everything someone might need to get started in the hobby, including things like a basic paint set, brushes, craft knives, etc. You could then advertise this specific kit in order to get people to visit your store, where they are likely to purchase other items.

❖ **Differ your business model** – A lot of people change their business model from the standard shopping cart type website to a subscription model, bundle model, or some other model. Just be sure whatever type of model you choose is suitable for YOUR market before you invest too much time and money into it.

Do not create a USP just for the sake of having one. Make sure it is suitable for your market and adds true value to the experience for your customer.

# Social Media

You probably already know how powerful social media can be for marketing purposes, but you might not know which sites would be most effective, or how to use each site for the most traffic and the best quality traffic. So let's talk a little about some of the popular networks, and how you can use them to get traffic AND sales.

## Facebook

Facebook is one of the most well-known social media platforms in the world. According to Statista, Facebook has over 2 billion monthly active users. Not just 2 billion accounts, but active users! They also have one of the most diverse audiences, with a greater number of mature users in addition to younger users.

Marketing on Facebook can happen in three major ways:

❖ Facebook pages

❖ Facebook groups

❖ Facebook ads

It is a good idea to set up a Facebook page for your business so you can start building your brand's presence there, but aside from using it for paid marketing, I would not focus too much attention on the page itself.

This is because Facebook has changed the way posts on pages appear on people's newsfeeds, resulting in far fewer views.

Instead, focus most of your efforts on building a Facebook GROUP.

Group posts are seen much more often, and groups also inspire more interaction than pages. Inside your group, you can hold members-only contests, giveaways, and more. This will encourage more people to join your group and be active in it.

You still need a page for advertising purposes because Facebook ads require this. And you can still post to the page regularly. But you should focus more effort on building your group in order to take advantage of the free traffic they can bring.

Facebook is probably the best overall social media platform for marketers, because the group function is incredibly powerful when used correctly, and because they have the most diverse audience when it comes to balance between the genders as well as covering the majority of age ranges, and other demographics.

## Instagram

Instagram has a user base that is mostly under 35, but they do still have a lot of users in other age ranges, too. This makes them another platform that is fairly diverse, but it is skewed to a mostly younger audience.

Instagram has recently been building a reputation as another great place for marketing because they have been working on their format in order to make it much more productive to advertisers without upsetting its core user base.

Because it is highly visual in nature, it makes it easy to market products by showing photos and videos that appeal to your market, and you can even demonstrate the product's use.

One thing that makes Instagram so powerful is that users are 58 times more likely to share a post than Facebook users, and 120 times more likely to do the same than Twitter users.

Instagram has also added a paid ad system that has been getting a lot of positive feedback. It is great for building brand awareness and engagement, but since the platform does not allow clickable links, it is not as effective for direct selling.

## Pinterest

Pinterest is not really considered a social network by a lot of people. It does have a social aspect, because you share content, which is viewed and shared by other people, and you can like and comment. However, it is not as robust in the social area as other networks. But we will include it here because it does work quite similarly to social networks.

Pinterest is widely considered one of the most effective platforms not only for getting traffic, but for getting sales, too. Analytics have shown Pinterest to be far more effective than most other platforms when it comes to marketing products.

Pinterest has a paid advertising system, too, and many marketers have found it to be remarkably powerful for generating sales.

The targeting is robust, and you can reach exactly the people you want to reach with exactly the products they are looking for.

## Other Social Networks

There are other networks that may or may not work for you, depending on your market and how you use them. For example, Twitter works very well for some people, and not so well for others. Snapchat can be excellent for younger, more tech-savvy markets, but possibly not as well for others.

It is a good idea to have a presence on many different networks, but do not spend too much time on them unless you really believe they have potential for YOUR market.

For example, LinkedIn advertising is reported to be quite effective, but it works mainly for a B2B audience, or when you are selling something that relates to education or job hunting.

If you want more in depth information on marketing your e-commerce store, check out Ecom Smart Start. You will learn a lot more ways to market your store to get the most traffic possible.

# Conclusion

If you have always wanted to open your own online store, but did not think you could make it happen, I hope you have changed your mind. It is a lot easier than you probably thought to get started.

In this guide, we have talked about how to choose a niche market, how to source products, and how to market your store. We have covered a lot of information, but there is still a lot we cannot possibly cover in a short report like this one.

If you want more detailed information on how to set up and run your ecommerce store, I highly recommend Ecom Smart Start.

You will learn such cool tactics as how to craft descriptions for your products that will turn tire-kickers into paying customers, how to get more stuff done quicker, how to use paid advertising effectively, and tons more.

I wish you the best of luck with your new store!

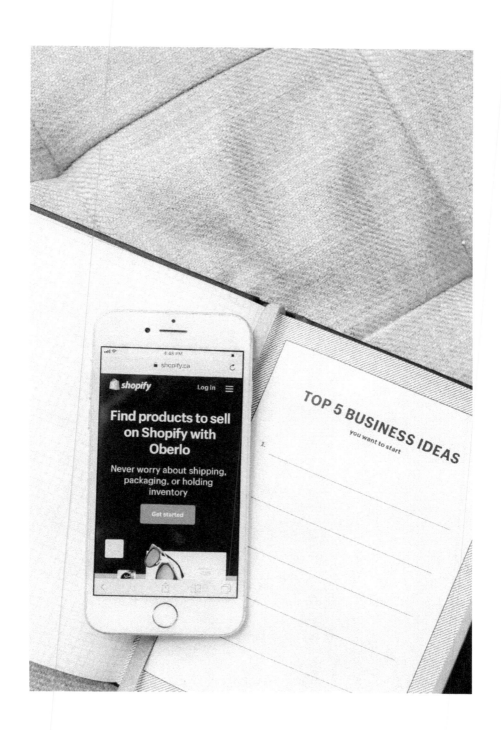